LETS
GO
PUBLISH!

How to End DACA, Sanctuary Cities, & Resident Illegal Aliens

A great Americans-first plan which saves US $Trillions. Learn how!

Countries as far away as Australia have problems with illegal aliens creating big issues for its citizens. The Aussies use a technique called the Assisted Voluntary Return as part of an overall Pay-to-Go plan to incent migrants to leave Australia and go back home. Pay-to-Go across the world pays both travel expenses and offers a generous stipend for those who sign up for the offer to return home. The same approach would work in the USA

But, what about those who would not leave the USA under any circumstance regardless of the incentive? Are we better off with the remainder of 60 million illegal interlopers staying in the shadows of America, rather than devising a plan to solve the problem in a way that keeps America whole and makes American citizens the masters of our own country again? I have devised such a plan. You will love it.

By solving the problem of illegal residents in the US—about 60 million at last count, a major side benefit when done the right way is that DACA is also solved as is the idea of Sanctuary Cities. One of the major advantages of this overall plan which I will call the Kelly Plan because my name is Kelly is that it was not created by inept Congressmen or inept Senators looking to get reelected. It was built by a guy just like you and so it is built to work. It is built to solve the problem. The solution is to provide a special visa for interlopers, renewable annually. Every year they are vetted when their required $100 + renewal application is processed. It is called the *Resident Visa*.

Interlopers never become citizens. They never vote. They collect no welfare or other freebies and Americans get jobs first. It is guaranteed to work if only we can get our legislators to pay attention to the fact that there is a great solution available today. No more shadows; No more DACA; No more Sanctuary Cities. How does that sound?. Besides all that, it will save the US a cool Trillion per year when it is fully implemented.

Congress tried in earnest to do something to solve the problem in 2013 with the Gang of Eight proposal. and they failed miserably. The people do not trust Congress because Democrats want the voters and Republicans want the workers. Regular people want their country back. Gang of Eight put them on a fast track to citizenship that would cost US taxpayers up to $6.3 Trillion with all of its provisions. In 2013, Americans told Congress and the House voted "no" and we sent the Gang of Eight Senators packing.

Our country is clearly in chaos; a race to the bottom in wages is underway; and regular Americans are losing the jobs and low-wages war every day. Trump is doing his best but even he is not a magician. The one clear choice for those wishing to stay in America would be if we can legalize interlopers on American terms with no benefits. This would end the sanctuaries and the shadows and be good for everybody. I think we can do it.

In this book, you will learn how. The plan takes interlopers out of the shadows and gives them the opportunity they seek while keeping Americans whole and keeping the country prospering. You're going to like this America-first plan built by an American for Americans.

BY

Brian W. Kelly

Title: **How to End DACA, Sanctuary Cities, & Resident Illegal Aliens.**
Copyright © 2017   *Brian W. Kelly*
Publisher: Brian P. Kelly
Author   Brian W. Kelly
Subtitle: *A great Americans-first plan--Saves US $Trillions. Learn how!*

Referenced Material:
Standard Disclaimer: The information in this book has been obtained through personal and third-party observations, interviews, and copious research. Where unique information has been provided or extracted from other sources, those sources are acknowledged within the text of the book itself or at the end of the chapter in the Sources Section. Thus, there are no formal footnotes nor is there a bibliography section. Any picture that does not have a source was taken from various sites on the Internet with no credit attached. If resource owners would like credit in the next printing, please email publisher.

Published by: LETS GO PUBLISH!
Editor   Brian P. Kelly
Email: info@letsgopublish.com
Web site   www.letsgopublish.com

Library of Congress Copyright Information Pending

Book Cover Design   Brian W. Kelly
Publisher   Brian P. Kelly

ISBN Information: The International Standard Book Number (ISBN) is a unique machine-readable identification number, which marks any book unmistakably. The ISBN is the clear standard in the book industry. 159 countries and territories are officially ISBN members. The Official ISBN For this book 978-1-947402-63-8

The price for this work is: $5.95 USD

10   9   8   7   6   5   4   3   2   1

Release Date: October 2018

Dedication

I would like to dedicate this book to my immediate family.

My wife Pat helps me more than I deserve as do my adult children, Brian, Michael, and Katie.

I love them all and that keeps me going.

The family would all be upset with me if I did not include our other little man, Buddie (Budmund).

He is the family CAT. He is a great one.

Acknowledgments:

I appreciate all the help that I have received in putting this book together as well as all the other 179 books from the past.

My acknowledgments were so large at one time that readers complained that they had to go through too many pages to get to page one of the book.

And, so in response, I put my acknowledgment list online, and it continues to grow. Believe it or not, it costs about a dollar less to print my books today than then. No kidding!

Thank you, my dear friends and supporters of many years. May God bless you all for your help.

You may check out www.letsgopublish.com to read the latest version of my heartfelt acknowledgments updated for this book.

A new lover of literature, Wily Ky Eyely continues her supportive efforts.

Thank you all very much!

Brian

Preface:

What would you call a plan that solved a problem for America that most of the Congress seems to have no interest in solving? I have called it many things while perfecting this book, but now let me settle my mental rumblings with what it should be called *The Resident Visa Plan*. It has a companion plan called the *Pay-to-Go Plan*. The implementation of both of these programs by the US government plus the building of the wall, solves the problem of 60 million illegal residents in America in a way that makes everybody happy.

This book, *How to End DACA, Sanctuary Cities, & Resident Illegal Aliens* is written in summary form so that it can be read quickly without sacrificing the essence of the plan. It is the ninth book on illegal immigration that I have written as I am trying to perfect an already good idea on how to solve this huge problem for Amrica.

This book and several of its predecessors that you can read at amazon.com/author/brianwkelly should be required reading for every House and Senate member as well as the President of the United States. This is the only plan that can work for Americans first to end the shadows and the sanctuaries and DACA and save America about a $Trillion per year. Kelly books are available on the Amazon and Barnes & Noble sites.

The most innovative of the plans is known as the Resident Visa Plan. It is a vision for a secret sauce solution to fix the problem of 60 million interlopers waking up in America every day without our permission. Yes—build the wall, please! But simultaneously solve the residence problem of so many people who do not belong here in America.

Do we really need up to 60 million interlopers in residence? I do not think so. Hey, John McCain, RIP, calculated over 128 million interlopers in residence. Maybe he was right. Do we need 128 Million? Can anybody tell me what we need? My personal thoughts are that we need zero. It is time to give Americans an opportunity to work in America for a much more than decent wage.

I am very pleased that you are reading this book and I hope many others find it and convince the US Administration and the Congress and the President that it is their turn to learn about The Resident Visa Plan and its companion plan, Pay-to-Go!. This idea should have been obvious without me, a guy from no place giving Congress, the US Senate, and the President a good idea.

The Resident Visa solution is unique, and everything needed to implement it is already in place. It directly addresses the issues that having 60 million illegal foreign nationals in residence have brought upon America. Nobody likes deportation but just like you would immediately throw an uninvited guest out of your house, it would be very fair for the US to throw out (deport) the 60 million uninvited guests in America today.

Yes, deportation is fair of course as these folks have broken our laws. But, our politicians are culpable as they made it too easy for foreigners to break our laws. The problem is that we do not see them in our house every day and so most of us have no stomach for deporting them.

Therefore, an adjunct solution to the *Resident Visa Plan* is the *Pay-to-Go Plan*. The US will pay the return expenses for each illegal interloper who chooses to return to their home country. Moreover, depending on their status in the USA, the government will provide a generous stipend of anywhere from $20,000 to $50,000 once they return. That's a good deal.

Amnesty is not a solution as Americans have already paid a big price for the largesse of politicians wanting low wages and those wanting the future votes of today's interlopers.

Ideally, the solution would be to go poof, and every foreign interloper would be taken back to where and when they crossed the border years and years ago.

Every plan requires fine tuning and we would expect this to continue to be the case with the Resident Visa Plan. When illegal interlopers do not want to be paid to go, and they want to stay in the US, the Resident Visa Plan comes in very handy. Together these plans are the long-sought solution to 60 million illegals in America. Nobody will be illegal and there will be no need for DACA or sanctuary citizens. Likewise, nobody from foreign lands will have a free ride anymore on the taxpayers. Both plans end this practice. Moreover, when implemented, the lights will be on and there will be no shadows. We will know where they all live

A key element of this plan is that each year the clock resets on foreign nationals who are permitted here on a temporary basis under the Resident Visa Plan. This book thus focuses on interlopers signing up to become Resident Visa Holders with appropriate renewal assurances for good behavior.

In summary, this book presents the Resident Visa Plan as the fix and the Pay-to-Go Plan as the backup fix. Then it offers many other points on why this is the one and only fix to create an America without shadows that favors Americans 100%. There is so much good left over that good-willed interlopers have a lot to gain simply by registering (signing up.)

You are going to love this book as well as the plans themselves. All interlopers immediately are to be registered and accountable. You will see that The Resident Visa Plan is designed by an American for Americans.

Additionally, illegal foreign nationals will be very pleased because the plan uses deportation as a very last resort and it immediately gets illegal foreign nationals out of the shadows. Few books are a must-read but *How to End DACA, Sanctuary Cities, & Resident Illegal Aliens* will quickly appear at the top of America's most read list.

This is a simple, America-first solution but only if Congress and the President have the guts! It solves the problem with 60 million interlopers in America and it offers an opportunity to solve the problem with visa overstays. Green cards, Anchor babies and other issues that plague Americans.

Sincerely,

Brian P. Kelly, Editor

Table of Contents

About the Author

Brian W. Kelly retired as an Assistant Professor in the Business Information Technology (BIT) program at Marywood University, where he also served as the IBM i and midrange systems technical advisor to the IT Faculty. Kelly has designed, developed, and taught many college and professional courses. He is also a contributing technical editor to a number of IT industry magazines, including "The Four Hundred" and "Four Hundred Guru" published by IT Jungle.

Kelly is a former IBM Senior Systems Engineer and he was a candidate for US Congress from Pennsylvania. He has an active information technology consultancy. He is the author of 179 other books, in many topical areas, as well as hundreds of articles. Kelly has been a frequent speaker at many US conferences. Invite him to your next conference on immigration solutions.

When Brian ran for Congress as a Democrat against a 13-term Democrat in 2010, he took no campaign contributions, spent just enough to buy signs and T-shirts, and as a virtual unknown. Yet, he captured 17% of the vote. Kelly says: "Writing books is lots easier than running for public office!"

Chapter 1 Is There a Solution for Resident Aliens in the US Shadows?

60 million interlopers cost many taxpayer dollars

If we knew how to immediately stop the drain on our government treasury with one bold and very fair move, would America's inept politicians make that move? I have done many analyses over none prior books, and I have concluded that American politicians, from Congress and the Senate on down, will never support Americans unless convinced that they would be out of office otherwise.

Based on what it costs to support illegal foreign nationals (average of $30,000 per person per year), the US can certainly afford to deport millions of people who are here illegally. But, the dirty politicians and the corrupt press preach a different mantra that puts Americans last and illegal aliens first. Democrats want more illegal voters and Republicans want to please their donors with cheap labor.

This book is written to solve the problem for regular Americans and that is why it will be so difficult to make it happen. Americans must toughen up and not give any representative another day in office if they do not adopt this sure-fire way to put American Citizens first. After all, this is America, not South America.

Ironically, though Americans complain about all of the illegal aliens, supporting them, having them take their jobs, and lowering the average wages in America, most would prefer a different solution than rounding them up and deporting 60 million people. But, we can afford deportation if we choose. If nobody was collecting welfare, this would be a lot tougher, and if nobody in illegal status was stealing from Americans, maybe no American would care. Americans are being played for patsies and our legislators are knowingly permitting it to happen.

Can we afford a mass deportation of illegal foreign nationals—even without a roundup? Yes, we can if we choose to, but the Kelly plan gives us a great option without deporting any good people.

Is there a consensus for or against the idea of deportation? It only matters if the US can actually afford to undertake a mass deportation?

Let me prove that we can afford deportation before we move on to solutions that we can stomach. I am not recommending mass deportation but we can certainly afford it and the US can save lots of money if we choose some day to do it.

Let's say that 30 million of the 60 million illegal aliens in residence, using fake ids which are very prevalent in the illegal resident community, collect some form of welfare from the US. This helps them afford their lives in America. What does that cost us citizens per year?

The cost per year is $30,000 X 30,000,000 = $900 Billion per year
The cost of deportation is $10,000 X 30 million = $300 Billion one time

The first-year savings is a net of $600 Billion after deportation. The second and subsequent years, the savings would be the full $900 Billion per year

Rather than look at the unpleasant task of coerced deportation, many countries across the world have instituted what they call *Pay-to-Go* programs in which a free return and a stipend incentive are offered to the migrants to induce them to return home. In our country we would be incenting illegal interlopers living in the shadows of America to go back home. US citizens would pay for their trip and bankroll them once they got there.

A very nice stipend amount that would persuade many interlopers to return to their home country is $20,000. In this way, the deportation is really a voluntary emigration back to the home country.

The cost of the stipend at $20,000 X 30,000,000 = $600 Billion one time. This is if the country is the USA.

In this example, the cost of the return and the cost of the stipend would be $900 billion if every interloper agreed to return home and then made good on their promise.

This is the same amount as the cost to support an interloper in the US for one year. The difference between the two is the savings. In year 1, in this scenario, the savings would be zero dollars and the cost would be zero dollars. In year two an annual savings of $900 billion would begin to accrue. Where does the savings come from? It comes from the US not having to pay welfare to illegals as well as Americans being able to get jobs that pay substantially more than when the interlopers were depressing wages by accepting sub-minimum wage positions.

Suppose the Pay-to-Go stipend were raised to $50,000, to attract more takers, the annual savings of as much as $900 billion would begin to accrue in year three so the stipend could be paid for. After year three, the US would be in the black on the program. My opinion is that $20,000 is a handsome enough fee.

Talk to your Congress

I predict that the biggest obstacle in solving the problem of 60 million illegal interlopers in America will be both chambers of the US Congress. I have presented this whole plan to Lou Barletta, running for the US Senate v Bob Casey, a twelve-year lifer who does not represent the people of Pennsylvania. Jr. Casey Jr. wants nothing to do with it and Lou Barletta is still conferring with his advisors. It is risky to propose something that the others in the US Senate may think is wrong. I hope Lou Barletta comes down on the side of the people.

I have also presented this whole plan to John Chrin, running for the House of Representatives v Matt Cartwright, a six-year lifer wannabe who does not represent the people of Northeastern Pennsylvania. Jr. Cartwright wants nothing to do with the resident visa or the Pay-To go as it interferes with his plan to permit illegal aliens to vote. Chrin is still conferring with his advisors. It is risky to propose something that the other Republicans in the House may think is wrong. I hope John Chrin comes down on the side of the people. It would help him defeat Matt Cartwright for sure.

I am not naïve enough to suggest that the current Congress' predilection for more voters and lower wages for all Americans could be overcome by the fact that this plan to deal with resident interlopers is the best yet conceived. So, if they remain recalcitrant, we may be forced to replace the entire Congress in order to do the right thing for America.

John McCain, RIP, was known for his personal estimate of about 4 million per year jumping the border. He was talking about Illegal aliens, which we like to refer to as illegal interlopers. An interloper is another word for an uninvited guest.

McCain's estimate was about those who have chosen to cross the southern border. In his estimate, he does not include the million or more a year who simply decide not to go home when their visas expire. So, the rate of illegals becoming a burden on US citizens is actually higher than MCain's original 4 million per year estimate.

Instead the visa-overstayers, who mostly came on student visas, opt for illegal residency in the US after they snag a job that should have gone to a recent American citizen graduate from a college or university. That's how we got into this problem in the first place. We did not invite 60 million people to America to sponge off US taxpayers. However, some of our elite representatives may very well have done exactly that.

US. amnesty advocate John McCain was a recognized authority on the subject of illegal immigration. In a letter dated February 2004, he wrote that apprehension figures demonstrated that "almost four million people crossed the US border illegally in 2002."

McCain estimated over 10,000 cross every day. If it were exactly 10,000, then 3,650,000 per year would be his estimate. Instead he simply rounded it up to 4 million. That comes to 128 million from 1986, the year of the Reagan amnesty to the end of 2017. If we cut that in half and round it down, we're looking at my long-time estimate of 60 million interlopers in residence today. I know that nobody can prove me wrong on that number.

The purpose of this book is to find a solution to the big problem of having 60 million illegal interlopers (uninvited guests) permanently enshrined in an illegal status in the United States today. There are three International plans implemented in a number of countries such as Australia to help migrants(illegal aliens in our US situation) return to their home countries. They are as follows:

1. Assisted Voluntary Return (AVR)
2. Assisted Voluntary Return & Reintegration (AVRR)
3. Pay-to-Go

The plans are self-descriptive. AVRR programs work with the governments in the home country so that after the return, the migrant can reintegrate with society in his or her country. This is a great idea. Pay-To-Go encompasses any plan that pays anything such as transportation costs home, reintegration costs, and/or stipends to induce interlopers or migrants to choose to return home.

There is no question that incenting a mass exodus from a country overcrowded with non-citizen migrants, legal or illegal, without the need for deportation can be a very effective way to again gain control of the illegal immigration situation in the United States.

In our country. I would recommend that the US implement a comprehensive Pay-to-Go program as soon as possible. Otherwise, the raw numbers of interlopers that are increasing every year will eventually bankrupt the US.

Generally, a citizen of a foreign country who wishes to enter the United States must first obtain a visa, either a nonimmigrant visa for a temporary stay, or an immigrant visa for permanent residence. For the most part, immigrant visas that are approved for permanent residence result in green cards.

Temporary visas for travel are easy to get. In 2016, for example, well over 10 million such visas were issued. In 2017, it is expected that there will be 11 million temporary visas issued. Since many countries are not required to produce visas, the numbers coming in are substantially higher, more like 60 to 70 million passports needed no visas to get into America. The USCIS is not very good in making sure that when there time is up, they go home. That, of course is why you are reading this book. It is not right.

What about legal immigration?

About 1.2 million green cards were issued in 2017. In 2014, a total of 1,016,518 persons became lawful permanent residents aka, LPRs complete with green card status. Over half of the new LPRs (53 percent) already lived in the United States when they were granted lawful permanent residence. Sixty-four percent of the new LPRs were granted lawful permanent resident status based on a family relationship with a U.S. citizen or lawful permanent resident of the United States. The leading countries of birth of new LPRs were Mexico (13 percent), India (7.7 percent), and China (7.5 percent)

The other type of legal resident in the US is known as a birthright citizen, colloquially known as an anchor baby.

If the stipend is a little higher, the Pay-to-Go Program could save the US another ton of funds if it were also used to attract green card holders on welfare, and anchor babies on welfare. When and if they agreed to return to their home countries there would no longer be a cost for their welfare. Think of what the US could do with another half trillion or as much as a full trillion dollars per year to spend on American interests?

The three categories for which the program could be used to include would be the following:

1. Current interlopers
2. Legal green card holders on welfare
3. Anchor babies at any age

The recommended stipend for each of the three categories would be as follows:

1. Current Interlopers $20,000
2. Legal Green Card Holders on Welfare $30,000
3. Anchor Babies or Adults $50,000

Anybody opting for a stipend in any of the above categories would be prohibited without special petition from ever returning to the United States for any reason. Any debt accrued that is accounted for in the Accountability System, explained in several of my books, would need to be collected prior to any request for readmission to be examined.

There are 15 million legal immigrants (green card holders) currently in the country. Half of them are on welfare. 7.5 million X $30,000 = $225 Billion per year.This is not an estimate. This is a fact. Why should Americans pay for those in line to be citizens? Because Congress does not want to upset our "guests." So, we know what we must ultimately do with our Congress.

There are 6 million birthright citizens (former anchor babies) born to illegal aliens currently in the country. They are almost all on welfare 6 million X $30,000 = $180 Billion per year. They show up on normal welfare roles because they are citizens.

The US can thus save an additional $405 Billion per year by adding the above two categories to the illegal interlopers able to use the Pay-to Go program or any other program that reduces costs to zero. This would make a total of three categories for which the program could be used.

What problem does the Pay-to Go program fix? It is a pro-America and pro-American citizen solution. It is an America-First solution to the major problem of 60 million illegal residents sponging off the taxpayers in the United States. Why do they think it is OK for them to do this? Our corrupt legislators encourage them to do so.

Once in the continental US, the interlopers either wholly or partially depend on US taxpayer dollars for their daily sustenance. Is your wallet looking a little thinner these days? The problem we plan to solve in this book, *the real problem,* is that 60 million illegal foreign nationals cost Americans money every day. They just don't pay their way and live here. They take from US.

This is more than enough of an introduction to both the problem and the solution. For those who would like to learn more about the programs besides the introduction here and the review in the second and last chapter, feel free to take the link to https://www.amazon.com/dp/194740217X.

Chapter 2 Should We Send 60 Million Interlopers Back Home?

Maybe!!!

Maybe we should send them back if that is what they want. It is my contention that we lured them into America by giving them the idea that the streets were paved with gold and when they took their share of that gold, the streets would grow more gold. They are culpable for sure but our politicians deceived them by not building a wall and by not enforcing our border protections.

Because of the role of corrupt American politicians in their coming here, there was an implicit promise that illegal interlopers could stay and we Americans would make sure that they were OK. Because of America's role in bringing them here, I would say that we owe them at least a free trip home with a little pocket money. But, we can afford a lot more and it would serve us well if we paid it.

Yes, you heard me right. We need to pay for their return 100% and give them some pocket money. We already estimated the cost to taxpayers in this chapter of a full-boat fake-id welfare recipient in 2017 at about $30,000 per year. We also calculated the savings of giving interlopers, green card holders, and anchor babies a large sum to go home. If the US were a business, it would be very prudent to institute a Pay-to-Go program.

I have written a complete book titled *Pay-to-Go*, available on Amazon that explores all of the details of the proposed US *Pay-to-Go* program. It is a great program and the US can afford it and it would benefit all Americans. Feel free to read the Pay-to-Go book for more information.

Both the Pay-to-Go and another program which we are about to discuss must be instituted together in the US for us to solve the problem of 60 million interlopers in residence in the shadows of America.

The fact is that not everybody will be willing to leave and return even though they would be returning to their homes.

Chapter 3 What If an Illegal Interloper Does Not Want to Return Home?

Countries of Origin: 2012 ProCon

Which 10 countries do 85% of the 11.4 million immigrants living in the United States illegally come from?

6.72 million from Mexico

1.17 million from Asia

1.78 million from Central and South America

59%

5%

3%

6%

1%

2%

2%

2%

3%

1%

Can anything be less appealing than the shadows?

A reasonable estimate is that with a $20,000 stipend, between 20% and 50% of the 60 million illegal aliens residing in America would take the money and return to their homes. Why would they want to persist in the shadows living in squalor, when they could get a great start with a big hunk of money back in their own country?

What we as a country would not want if we put forth a program to solve the problem is for just 20% of the problem to be solved. We might have 80% of the illegal residents remaining in the shadows. Then what? Would we even notice the improvement?

If illegal interlopers choose to stay in America, we have to make that OK or we wind up like today with shadows, sanctuary cities, and too many bad guys with a place to hide. However, the terms must favor Americans. To get out of the shadows, any illegal interloper would be required to agree to those terms.

The US savings on the Pay-to-Go as we proved is huge and it is easy to calculate. After the first year it is $30,000 per alien who returns per year. Not having to pay $30,000 per illegal alien is like making $30,000 extra. Over a lifetime, that would save taxpayers $1.8 million per person. Multiply $30,000 by 60,000,000 by 60 years to get $108 trillion in total possible savings? How can Congress say no?

Now what if we let them stay here legally rather than in sanctuary cities and in the shadows? How would that be good for Americans? The Resident Visa program is designed for an America-first country. It can produce the same savings one year sooner than Pay-to-Go as there is no cost at all for this program. All program costs are paid by the resident visa holders. I am sure you want to hear more about this

I don't want to go home, period!

If a resident illegal foreign national really does not want to go home and would rather live in the shadows or in sanctuary in Chicago, regardless of the cash incentive to return home, should Americans simply accept that as the end of negotiations? Without another program that fits, we would continue to be stuck in America with shadows and an underground economy, and a ton of illegal interlopers tapping the welfare system with fake stolen identification—perhaps using your social security number.

Desperate people do desperate things. Who wants 60 million desperate people living next door? Nobody in America would think the problem is solved if that is all that remains from the Pay-to-Go proposition.

There is no amnesty in this deal

There is always another option. This one actually costs US taxpayers nothing and it permits the interloper who will not go home, to stay in America indefinitely in a temporary legal status as long as they "behave." The big differences between this and the shadows and sanctuary cities is that the shadows and sanctuaries are completely gone and will be illegal.

The big difference between this and amnesty is that there is no welfare for Resident Visa Holders, and there is no green card to make the visa holder a permanent resident on a path to citizenship. They are temporary visa holders and that is it. They are not half-citizens or semi-citizens or legal permanent residents or citizens. They are simply holders of a legal visa in the US. They have the same rights as any other temporary visa holder plus one more.

Each year, they can renew their temporary Resident Visa by paying a renewal fee and being vetted again. The former illegal interlopers become legal temporary residents with a $100 to $200 annual renewal depending on what is cost effective for Americans.

From a financial standpoint, each former interloper, in order to gain the benefits of no-shadows, must agree to participate in zero welfare programs. If the illegal interlopers cannot afford the financial demands of the Resident Visa program after ten years, they would still be able to participate in the Pay-to-Go program. They could return home voluntarily with a large stipend. New illegal aliens who break-in after the inception of the program would be deported immediately.

As a big benefit for Americans, the shadows and the sanctuaries would be gone completely. DACA would not be needed. Even former aliens would be registered in the system once they get their special "passport." US authorities would know how many there are and know for sure who they are. Multiply the number of illegal interlopers left after the completion of the Pay-to-Go program by the $30,000 per person per year savings to calculate the annual savings for this resident program. It is more than $500 Billion per year.

Since this system depends on working computer systems, we can use the same system for other visa holders so that they cannot get lost when their visas expire.

The US Immigration Department already issues millions of travel visas for potential interlopers from other countries on a temporary basis and they have a cost of about $140.

The US would need to assure that a system would be in place that would permit a one-year expiration on a Resident Visa and an option for an annual renewal for all 60,000,000 interlopers left behind after Pay-to-Go. If there is no renewal, deportation or coerced Pay-to-Go at the lowest stipend rate become the only options left.

After each year, the resident visa holder would be able to renew the Resident Visa for another year unless they have broken the terms of the arrangement. They will never vote. Without going home and reengaging in their home countries, they will never be citizens, and they will never cost the US a dime. And, they can never commit a crime or they will be deported immediately.

So, what I am proposing is that the program provides for granting interlopers in good standing what we should simply call a *Resident Visa*. This would be a new visa type that, unlike other visa types can be renewed each and every year with conditions.

With this, former illegal foreign nationals would be legalized under the protection of the Resident Visa. They could remain in America out of the shadows on a one-year renewable temporary basis as long as they behaved in a lawful manner according to the exact terms of their visa.

There are many differences between illegally gaining benefits in the United States and becoming legal by gaining a Resident Visa. Those choosing to employ the Resident Visa to stay in America, are welcome to do so for one year after the program begins. However, the terms of the relationship with US officials will not be the same as when they were illegal. No illegal aliens will be tolerated one year after the program commences. Additionally, after one-year, the illegal interlopers who do not obtain their visa, would have the option of coerced deportation or Pay-to-Go.

There will be a vetting process in order to initially be approved. The visa will be special in that it will be renewable with a fee of $100 to $200, required annually after a renewal application, a record update (demographics, etc.), and a re-vetting of the applicant, and an eventual special oath of allegiance and the requirement over two years to learn and to speak English.

There are major benefits to the former foreign national for going through this process. The Resident Visa holder will receive an official photo ID at their application source so they do not have to carry a passport or an accompanying visa.

For those familiar with the notion of American visas, this unique visa would permit those approved, to live in America as long as they want, on a temporary but renewable basis for as long as they want as long as they behave and they renew their Resident Visa each and every year.

In essence, this process provides a Resident Visa, which would be an official US visa. Like all other US Visas, this would provide all of the benefits of a US non-immigrant category visa and more.

Chapter 4 A Pro-American Comprehensive Immigration Program

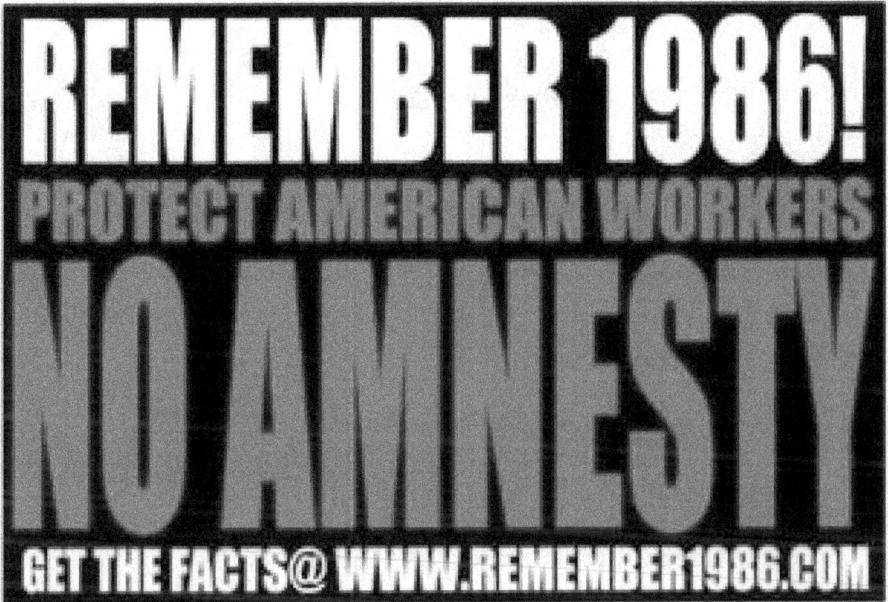

REMEMBER 1986!
PROTECT AMERICAN WORKERS
NO AMNESTY
GET THE FACTS@ WWW.REMEMBER1986.COM

Are words *comprehensive* and *American* incompatible?

We have already described the proposed Resident Visa Program and the Pay-to-Go program in simple terms. The-Gang-of-Eight Senators, made the term comprehensive a synonym of amnesty and as such it did not belong in the same sentence as American. Pay-to-Go and the Resident Visa are all-American notions that reflect the good-will of the American people in a genuinely comprehensive way. These programs together have all that is needed to solve the problem of DACA, the shadows and the sanctuaries forever.

Can this possibly be enough to prompt Congress and the President to finally create a *pro-American, comprehensive* immigration plan. Those normal and reasonable people who read the plan will know immediately that it will work and work well.

Overall, its acceptance depends on what's in it for Americans and what is in it for Illegal Foreign National Interlopers? Let's examine the benefits for interlopers first. Yes, a pro-American plan can have lots of great benefits for illegal foreign nationals.

Both programs together provide many benefits for those currently living in the shadows. For those wanting to stay in America now have a way to gain freedom to roam and a sense of belonging and an opportunity to succeed in America.

Think about why an illegal alien residing in America in the shadows should like the Resident Visa Program? While you are thinking, consider the seventeen points beginning on the next page:

1. No more living in the shadows of America.
2. Opportunity to go home travel-free if desired with a big stipend paid by Americans.
3. Resident Visa Holder (RVH) can get in line (back of line) in home country for citizenship without leaving US.
4. With renewals, the opportunity to live in America a lifetime.
5. Can obtain a driver's license, insurance, etc.
6. Can keep any job that is already held.
7. Can apply for any job available in America.
8. Can live wherever they want in America.
9. Can get same *paid by patient medical insurance* as Americans.
10. Can get installment loans from US Government on an exception basis to help with medical and educational expenses. Must be paid back.
11. After ten years but no more, living with a Resident Visa, can still opt for Pay-to-Go.
12. Green Card Pay-to Go stipend of $30,000 per permanent resident.
13. Anchor person Pay-to-Go huge stipends of $50,000 per birthright citizen.
14. Green Card Resident Visa stipend of $30,000 per permanent resident for transition from permanent residency to Resident Visa.
15. Anchor citizen Resident Visa stipend of $50,000 per birthright citizen) for transition from citizen to Resident Visa.

As you can see, we included some of the benefits of the Pay-to-Go program in the list above.

Many of the advantages for current interlopers are listed in the points above. The Pay-to-Go program provides a stipend that is more generous than any other country in the world. The Resident Visa Program immediately gets interlopers out of the shadows and provides a stipend for green card holders and anchor citizens who transition from their current program to the Resident Visa Program with the option after ten years of using Pay-to-Go.

If you want to stay in America, the Resident Visa is the best plan for illegal interlopers. If you want to stay in America and receive a generous stipend, the Resident Visa transition can also be used by Green Card Holders as well as Anchor Citizens.

Knowing this is so beneficial to interlopers, why should an American find it acceptable? The answer is simple. Americans are smart and upon analysis they can see that both plans if implemented by Congress and/or the President will save a ton of dollars for all American taxpayers. Moreover, nobody really likes DACA, the shadows or the sanctuaries.

Many Americans do not trust the government, period. So, why would Americans think this is a good deal if the illegal foreign national does not choose to exit America with a stipend? Then what?

If an illegal foreign national chooses not to accept this US government act of kindness, and does not go home, and does not sign up for The Resident Visa Program, the only option left is to stay in the shadows and/or sanctuaries. This will result in the interloper being asked to leave the country at their own expense or to accept the generous Pay-to-Go option.

By the enactment of this new visa and this new "Pay-to-Go" return home" plan, the idea of residing in America in an illegal alien status is being eliminated. The lack of a decision by an illegal interloper to choose one or the other will unfortunately provoke immigration authorities to deport them with no benefits.

Why should an American citizen like these two plans?

1. The days of the free lunch are over.
2. Both programs are cost free to Americans
3. Pay-to-Go stipends pay for themselves in one year
4. Illegal aliens must agree to terms of Resident Visa-- all benefits eliminated after 1st year.
5. Once an illegal alien returns home, cannot come back; no cost to Americans after year 1.
6. No more birthright citizenship for illegals, permanent residents, and Resident Visa Holders. Children born in America in future may apply for a Resident Visa.
7. No cash, medical services, education, welfare, or other benefits permitted for those with a Resident Visa.
8. Visa holders receive no citizen-only privileges.
9. Resident Visa Holders have no right to vote in any election.
10. New jobs must go to American citizens first—all things being equal.
11. Fees, fines on employers will help pay for Resident Visa program kickoff. Can generate as much as $400 Billion.
12. When program in high gear, US will save from 500 Billion dollars to One Trillion dollars per year on avoided interloper expenses.
13. Resident Visa holder must be employed.
14. Resident Visa holder must have health insurance.
15. Resident Visa holder must pass English test in two years
16. Resident Visa holder must take oath of allegiance to be approved for 1st renewal
17. No more green cards for family reunification-instead use Resident Visa.
18. All green card permanent residence visas are eliminated when expired. No new green cards. Use Resident Visa.
19. Next 10-yr green card renewal becomes a Resident Visa
20. No path to citizenship without going home to get in line (begin a process like all others from that country)
21. Citizenship line -- jumping the line is not permitted.
22. No more "need" for Sanctuary Cities
23. No more need for DACA Dreamers
24. Major cost savings for America

The end of Sanctuary Cities

Victor David Hanson writes: "Sanctuary cities protect illegal aliens from federal immigration agencies in a way that is not true of American citizens who arrive at airports and must go through customs, with no exemption from federal agents examining their passports and personal histories. If crimes or infractions are found, there is no safe space at an airport exempt from federal enforcement."

The new migrant programs that I am recommending either pay illegal interlopers to go or provide a Resident Visa that offers many benefits to both interlopers and American citizens. For example, it saves over $500,000,000 000 per year after year one of its implementation. With no more illegal aliens in the country, a major advantage is that the divisive notion of Sanctuary Cities and the term Sanctuary Cities can be removed from the US vocabulary. There will be no need for them with residents all being legal.

Anchor babies qualify

The Pay-to-Go Program is also available to those who became citizens through the anchor baby loophole of the 14th amendment. When an Anchor child with parent chooses to join the Pay-to-Go Program, each anchor citizen child will receive a $50,000 stipend and each of his or her interloper parents will receive their own $20,000 for a total of $70,000 for a two-person family and $90,000 for a three-person family with one anchor child. A family of four children with a mom or dad would receive $240,000. This is very affordable for US citizens considering the lifetime cost of one anchor baby can be as much as $2 million or more.

DACA "children" also qualify

The SRRV program solves the problem for DACA children also. DACA children qualify for the full $20,000 stipend in the Pay-to-Go Program. Those in the DACA program also qualify for the Resident Visa Program if they want to stay in the US. As an additional DACA concession for the "Children" who opt for the Resident Visa, there will be no charge for the visa for the first five renewal years. DACA "children" will be vetted when they apply for a resident passport. Gang members, of course, will be deported without benefits.

Green card holders also qualify

Green card holders, about 15,000,000 are legal permanent residents (LPR). Some are awaiting their time so they can be citizens. Others have chosen to stay legal in America without being citizens. Many are on welfare costing the US $30,000 each. Resident Green Card holders can receive a $30,000 stipend and use the Pay-to-Go option to return home, or they can receive a $30,000 stipend to downgrade their status from LPR to Resident Visa. Since Resident Visa holders do not receive welfare, this would save as much as several hundred billion dollars if all those in LPR status switched to Resident Visas or returned home.

Green card program can be eliminated

Because many in the LPR program collect welfare as an entitlement, I would recommend that the US eliminate green cards completely. All those who qualify to be citizens can be granted a Resident Visa and all other things for them would be the same. However, they would not be able to collect welfare with a Temporary visitors' visas. The US would save $Billions.

The evidence is on the table.

Nobody in their right mind wants life to continue with a shadow population who in many ways have been victimized similar to how slaves were victimized many years ago. The Pay-to-Go and the Resident Visa are programs that provide a way out of the mess for both interlopers and regular Americans.

Greedy fat cat business persons and politicians at the highest levels created this mess for both factions. Consequently, the plan includes substantial fees and fines for those businesses who hired illegal interlopers instead of Americans. Being greedy will collectively cost the fat cats over $400 Billion in total and perhaps more.

Companies made a ton of money off the backs of Americans with lower wages while poor interlopers were living in squalor earning sub-minimum wages. American industry as represented by the Chamber of Commerce should show some remorse and voluntarily chip in to help solve this problem and back the Pay-to-Go and the Residence Visa Programs as winner ideas for all decent Americans and the long-suffering communities whose only solace is the shadows of America.

Quick Comparison with the Gang of Eight

In 2013, you may recall that eight US Senators known as the Gang of Eight got a bill passed in the Senate that sold Americans down the river and would have given a ton of benefits to illegal aliens at taxpayer cost. The Pay-to-Go and the Resident Visa Programs are both pro-American and they save taxpayers substantial dollars. It is nothing like the John McCain / Marco Rubio Gof8 sellout. The following quick comparison chart is shown to help us better understand the new Resident Visa recommendation by comparing it in the chart below with the Gang of Eight Program which was passed by the US Senate.

| D: Charles Schumer- NY | D: Dick Durbin - IL | D: Robert Menendez -NJ | D: Michael Bennet - CO |
| R: John McCain - AZ | R: Lindsey Graham - SC | R: Jeff Flake - AZ | R: Marco Rubio - FL |

2013 Gang of Eight v Resident Visa

	G of 8	Resident Visa, PTG
Border secure	No	More technology
Jobs	Favors Interlopers	Favors Americans
Amnesty	Yes	No
Path to citizenship	Yes	No (almost same as today)
Permanent residents	Yes	Never, renewable visa
Voting	Yes	No, Never
Welfare benefits	Yes	No, Never
Freebies	Yes	No, Never
Anchor babies	Yes	No, stipends to return / change
Employer fees/fines	No	Yes -if one illegal employee
Reunification	33M in 10yrs	Not for Resident Visa Holders
Coerced-deportation	None	As needed for violations
Return to home country	No	Yes, with stipend
Must have healthcare	No	Yes
Must be employed	No	Yes
Must speak English in 2 yrs?	No	Yes
Oath of allegiance	No	Yes, after 1 year
Cost/debt accountability	No	Yes
Taxpayer Costs	$ 6Trillion	Zero
Payback plan	No	Yes
Accountability Database	No	Yes
Interloper fine	Yes	Yes
Employer fine	No	Yes (helps finance program)
Back taxes	No	Yes (vetting interviews)

The next chapter is part of a speech that your author previously sent out to Senate Candidate Lou Barletta, and House Candidate John Chrin. The objective is that, along with three other major platform points (Obamacare, Social Security COLA, and Student Debt), this major resident alien solution can make it easy for Republican Congressional and Senatorial candidates in America to understand and adopt a platform that solves the resident alien issue in America. It also can help attract good candidates who believe and can get elected.

Chapter 5 Solution Review: Pay-to-Go and Resident Visa

Do not trust that any US Congressman or any US Senator or any candidate for such office knows how to solve the immigration and illegal resident problem in America. There are only three solutions that will actually work. They must be executed in combination.

First, to stop those want to drop into America simply because they want to, whether they are good people or gang members, the President Trump border wall is a necessity for all Americans. Only foolish, anti-American Democrats suggest otherwise in their attempt to deceive the people of this great country.

There are two other pieces of the puzzle in this one winning platform point. Unlike the border wall, nobody speaks about this because it is still not known to the general public. That is why your author keeps writing and writing and writing. He has the solution but Congress will not embrace the right idea to solve the problem with illegal residency.

Illegal residents are those illegal foreign national interlopers who live in America and truly believe that the US Congress has given them a free pass to live in America and collect welfare. If that is true, what is not true is that the people of the US have not given the Congress permission to treat foreigners better than US citizens.

So, besides the Donald Trump border-wall, which is intended to stop the flow from the South into the United States, two new programs are necessary to remove and or legalize those illegal foreign nationals who today are living in the shadows or openly in US Sanctuary Cities. The objective of your author in this book and in other ways he has tried, is to solve illegal immigration, so it no longer exists in America.

Pay attention, please as the solution is so logical, that you won't believe that nobody besides your author, Brian Kelly with his *Kelly Plan* has yet to recommend it. The two major solution points defined are as follows:

1. Pay to Go
2. Resident Visa

As part of a four-point plan presented in many other Kelly books, this immigration solution can assure that a candidate for US Senate or for the House of Representatives can assure themselves a victory. The candidate must promise to sponsor legislation called for by their constituents. The essence of the legislation is presented in this book. Once every two or six years, these constituents are called voters by the election pundits.

60 million to 128 million living in US illegally

Checking history, you would find that in February 2004, the late and wise Arizona Senator John McCain recognized via Border Patrol reports that nearly four million people crossed our southern border "illegally" each year following the big Reagan amnesty in 1986. Nonetheless, the fraudulent press still insists that the total count of illegal immigrants residing in the United States is stagnant at eleven million, a mathematical impossibility if John McCain and Border Patrol figures are to be believed.

And McCain also understood that of these millions of foreigners, countless amounts, most using fake ID's, receive full welfare benefits while, contrary to popular mythology, very few actually work in agriculture.

There may be as many as 60 million and perhaps more illegal foreign nationals living in the United States today. Nobody can prove your author wrong on that number. While some individuals in this group may contribute to our society, on balance this is outweighed by the group's overall negative impact on the US. They drain the coffers of government assistance. They create lost employment opportunities for American citizens, and they commit a preponderance of criminal offenses as a percentage of their numers.

It is amazing how effective the fake-ID business is in turning illegal aliens into fake citizens who are thus enabled to enjoy American rights, benefits, and privileges.

Are Illegal Aliens All Criminals.

No, they are not all criminals as defined by those who do not count their illegal entry as a crime—even though it is against American law. But there is no illegal foreign national in America who has not broken US immigration law. When we talk about Crimianl Alien Statistics, however, we are looking at bigger crimes than crossing the border without a passport. By the way, try leaving your passport at home on your next trip to Mexico or Honduras or Aruba. See if you don't wind up in the hoosegow.

According to the 2011 GAO report entitled "Criminal Alien Statistics," the cost of crimes by illegal foreign nationals in 2011 was $8.1 billion per year, and that's without even considering the incomprehensibly larger emotional toll this problem takes on families whose priceless loved ones can never be replaced. I would estimate the cost today at $20 billion.

If elected, a candidate for Congress or the US Senate committed to solving the problem of illegal residents living in America would introduce two pieces of legislation that will solve this problem of illegal residents in the shadows—once and for all.

Besides many other benefits, it stands to save the U.S. over $1 Trillion per year in addition to a major reduction in crime. The two solutions are known as *pay-to-go* and the *resident visa*. They are real and not to be taken lightly. Let's look at them individually, so we all can understand how they solve the problem of illegal residency permanently. Perhaps even the proverbial Punxsutawney groundhog will never see his shadow again? But if it solves our problem with illegal residency in the US, it would it not be worth it?

Pay-to-Go

Most Americans are unaware that it costs taxpayers $30,000 per year on the average, per illegal alien in America to provide them with welfare benefits that would make them pleased enough to not complain to the New York Times. Each illegal resident and their dependent children, who sign up for Pay to Go, on the way back to the home country, will receive a one-time $20,000 stipend plus the individual expense of going back to the home country.

With a cost of $30,000 per year welfare cost to support unwelcome interlopers, drained from the US Treasury, a taxpayer savings of $10,000 begins year one and continues at $30,000 per year per person forever afterwards. This is not a bad deal for Americans and an even better deal for illegal alien interlopers. Americans owe them nothing but paying them one time to save dollars forever for US citizens is a good idea worth considering.

The program therefore quietly accommodates family reunification in the home country. Democrats won't call it family reunification, but it really is. If Democrats and the ACLU were permitted by their ideology to say this was a great idea, they would still be against it— but I cannot come up with a logical reason why?

A family of five for example, could do quite well back home after receiving $100,000 in stipends from Uncle Sam. Reuniting families in their own countries is a good idea for them and for America. Why would they want to live in a strange country when they could live like Kings in their own country?

For US taxpayers, to repeat, the savings in welfare means there would be no cost in year one and in year 2 and every year hence, the savings would equal $30,000 for each person who "goes." back home, never to return.

Moreover, there is no settling issue as the returnee to the home country knows how to live there and does not create an issue for their home country of record. e

Resident Visa

Because the US had chosen for years and years not to deport all interlopers for its own reasons (and Obama's reasons), those illegal interlopers, who would not leave the US under any circumstances under which they had control, have another option under this plan.

I believe that US citizens are kind to foreigners to offer both of these plans. An illegal interloper can sign up, be vetted, and eventually be approved for a *Resident Visa*. The visa will cost $200.00 in year 1, to cover vetting, and it will be renewable every year thereafter for a $100.00 to perhaps $150.00 renewal fee If the cost is more than $150.00, it will be increased appropriately. Their status is not permanent and there is no guarantee that a visa holder who misbehaves can stay in America. In fact, the contrary is true.

To get a *Resident Visa*, a former interloper would agree to all stipulations after registering. At the end of the registration process, US officials would know where every former illegal interloper is living. That is a major advantage as we do not have this information even today.

Stipulations would include full initial vetting; onsite renewal vetting; keep existing jobs; new jobs for Americans first; no voting; no citizenship; no welfare and no freebies of any kind.

Everybody would not be automatically approved for the *resident visa.* After vetting, those not approved for the resident visa program would automatically be enabled to use the *Pay-to-Go* program to aid in their relocation back to their home countries where they are known by all their friends. They would not be able to stay in America if not approved

As the program would, by definition, entail 100% participation from illegal residents, estimates are as high as $500 billion per year cost savings in total for those who choose to go or for those who choose to stay using the no-welfare *resident visa.* Another $500 billion will be reclaimed over time for the lost wages of Americans. Additionally, if we can figure a way for countries to reclaim their criminals, there is another $8.1 billion (2011 figures) to $20 billion (2018 estimate) to be recovered.

Once the program is in effect, there would be no more illegal aliens in the country. Would that not be nice? They would either be gone as a result of Pay-to-Go or they would be granted *Resident Visas.* Think of that as a major benefit. Everybody would be legal, and we would know who they are. They would all have agreed to no welfare benefits or they would have agreed to leave our country under the *Pay-to-Go plan.*

Because *Resident Visa* holders would be legal, the shadows would be eliminated. There would be no more shadows in America. There would be no need for DACA and no need for Sanctuary cities Let me repeat that.

All issues with DACA would be over and Sanctuary Cities would be a thing of the past because there would be no shadows and no illegal interlopers.

Ladies and gentlemen, that sounds like a solution that would work for illegal interlopers as well as American citizens. What do you think?

Other Books by Brian Kelly: (amazon.com, and Kindle)

Millennials Say America Was "Never That Great": Too many pleased days of political chumps not over!
White People Are Bad! Bad! Bad! In 2018, too many people find race as a non-equalizer.
It's Time for The John Doe Party… Don't you think? By By Elephants.
Great Players in Florida Gators Football… Tim Tebow and a ton of other great players
Great Coaches in Florida Gators Football… The best coaches in Gator history.
The Constitution by Hamilton, Jefferson, Madison, et al. The Real Constitution
The Constitution Companion. Will help you learn and understand the Constitution
Great Coaches in Clemson Football The best Clemson Coaches right to Dabo Swinney
Great Players in Clemson Football The best Clemson players in history
Winning Back America. America's been stolen and can be won back completely
The Founding of America… Great book to pick up a lot of great facts
Defeating America's Career Politicians. The scoundrels need to go.
Midnight Mass by Jack Lammers… You remember what it was like Great story
The Bike by Jack Lammers… Great heartwarming Story by Jack
Wipe Out All Student Loan Debt--Now! Watch the economy go boom!
No Free Lunch Pay Back Welfare! Why not pay it back?
Deport All Millennials Now!!! Why they deserve to be deported and/or saved
DELETE the EPA, Please! The worst decisions to hurt America
Taxation Without Representation 4th Edition Should we throw the TEA overboard again?
Four Great Political Essays by Thomas Dawson
Top Ten Political Books for 2018… Cliffnotes Version of 10 Political Books
Top Six Patriotic Books for 2018… Cliffnotes version of 6 Patriotic Boosk
Why Trump Got Elected!.. It's great to hear about a great milestone in America!
The Day the Free Press Died. Corrupt Press Lives on!
Solved (Immigration) The best solutions for 2018
Solved II (Obamacare, Social Security, Student Debt) Check it out; They're solved.
Great Moments in Pittsburgh Steelers Football... Six Super Bowls and more.
Great Players in Pittsburgh Steelers Football ,,,Chuck Noll, Bill Cowher, Mike Tomin, etc.
Great Coaches in New England Patriots Football,,, Bill Belichick the one and only plus others
Great Players in New England Patriots Football… Tom Brady, Drew Bledsoe et al.
Great Coaches in Philadelphia Eagles Football..Andy Reid, Doug Pederson & Lots more
Great Players in Philadelphia Eagles Football Great players such as Sonny Jurgenson
Great Coaches in Syracuse Football All the greats including Ben Schwartzwalder
Great Players in Syracuse Football. Highlights best players such as Jim Brown & Donovan McNabb
Millennials are People Too !!! Give US millennials help to live American Dream
Brian Kelly for the United States Senate from PA: Fresh Face for US Senate
The Candidate's Bible. Don't pray for your campaign without this bible
Rush Limbaugh's Platform for Americans… Rush will love it
Sean Hannity's Platform for Americans… Sean will love it
Donald Trump's New Platform for Americans. Make Trump unbeatable in 2020
Tariffs Are Good for America! One of the best tools a president can have
Great Coaches in Pittsburgh Steelers Football Sixteen of the best coaches ever to coach in pro football.
Great Moments in New England Patriots Football Great football moments from Boston to New England
Great Moments in Philadelphia Eagles Football. The best from the Eagles from the beginning of football.
Great Moments in Syracuse Football The great moments, coaches & players in Syracuse Football
Boost Social Security Now! Hey Buddy Can You Spare a Dime?
The Birth of American Football. From the first college game in 1869 to the last Super Bowl
Obamacare: A One-Line Repeal Congress must get this done.
A Wilkes-Barre Christmas Story A wonderful town makes Christmas all the better
A Boy, A Bike, A Train, and a Christmas Miracle A Christmas story that will melt your heart
Pay-to-Go   America-First Immigration Fix
Legalizing Illegal Aliens Via Resident Visas Americans-first plan saves $Trillions. Learn how!
60 Million Illegal Aliens in America!!! A simple, America-first solution.
The Bill of Rights By Founder James Madison Refresh *your knowledge of the specific rights for all*
Great Players in Army Football Great Army Football played by great players..
Great Coaches in Army Football Army's coaches are all great.
Great Moments in Army Football Army Football at its best.
Great Moments in Florida Gators Football Gators Football from the start. This is the book.
Great Moments in Clemson Football CU Football at its best. This is the book.
Great Moments in Florida Gators Football Gators Football from the start. This is the book.
The Constitution Companion. A Guide to Reading and Comprehending the Constitution

The Constitution by Hamilton, Jefferson, & Madison – Big type and in English
PATERNO: The Dark Days After Win # 409. Sky began to fall within days of win # 409.
JoePa 409 Victories: Say No More! Winningest Division I-A football coach ever
American College Football: The Beginning From before day one football was played.
Great Coaches in Alabama Football Challenging the coaches of every other program!
Great Coaches in Penn State Football the Best Coaches in PSU's football program
Great Players in Penn State Football The best players in PSU's football program
Great Players in Notre Dame Football The best players in ND's football program
Great Coaches in Notre Dame Football The best coaches in any football program
Great Players in Alabama Football from Quarterbacks to offensive Linemen Greats!
Great Moments in Alabama Football AU Football from the start. This is the book.
Great Moments in Penn State Football PSU Football, start--games, coaches, players,
Great Moments in Notre Dame Football ND Football, start, games, coaches, players
Cross Country with the Parents A great trip from East Coast to West with the kids
Seniors, Social Security & the Minimum Wage. Things seniors need to know.
How to Write Your First Book and Publish It with CreateSpace
The US Immigration Fix--It's all in here. Finally, an answer.
I had a Dream IBM Could be #1 Again The title is self-explanatory
WineDiets.Com Presents The Wine Diet Learn how to lose weight while having fun.
Wilkes-Barre, PA; Return to Glory Wilkes-Barre City's return to glory
Geoffrey Parsons' Epoch... The Land of Fair Play Better than the original.
The Bill of Rights 4 Dummmies! This is the best book to learn about your rights.
Sol Bloom's Epoch ...Story of the Constitution The best book to learn the Constitution
America 4 Dummmies! All Americans should read to learn about this great country.
The Electoral College 4 Dummmies! How does it really work?
The All-Everything Machine Story about IBM's finest computer server.
ThankYou IBM! This book explains how IBM was beaten in the computer marketplace by neophytes

Amazon.com/author/brianwkelly
Brian W. Kelly has written 180 books. Thank you for buying this one.

www.ingramcontent.com/pod-product-compliance
Lightning Source LLC
Chambersburg PA
CBHW060656280326
41933CB00012B/2209